Rain Dance

BY
Alice Gomez & Marilyn Rife

FOR
Marimba

RAIN DANCE

(For an added optional effect, wrist bells may be worn throughout this piece.)

ST-695

ALICE GOMEZ
MARILYN RIFE

♩ = 92

Solo Marimba

ST-695

3

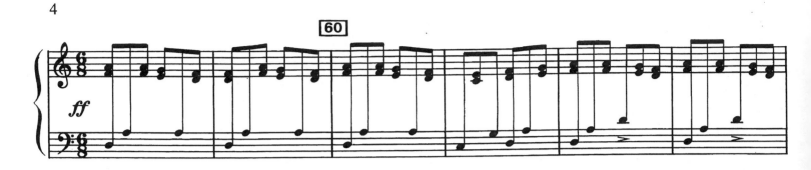

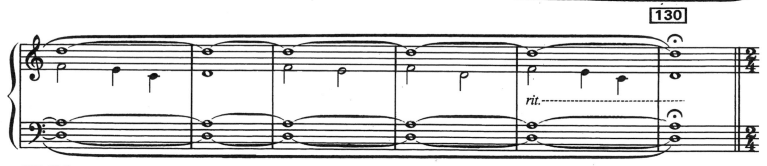

Tempo I

Selected Marimba Publications

SOLO, UNACCOMPANIED

BACH, C.P.E.
Brody, Sharda

ST454   Solfeggio in c Minor (Grade 4)

BACH, J.S.
Stoltzman, Mika

SU826   Chaconne for Marimba (Grade 5)

This Chaconne is the final movement from Johann Sebastian Bach's Partita No. 2 in D minor for solo violin, BWV 1004. It was composed in between 1717-1720. Some have suggested that the Chaconne, a theme and variations that lasts as long as the first four movements combined, was a tombeau written in memory of Bach's first wife, Maria Barbara, who died in 1720. There is no doubt, however, that the work stands as a towering achievement, a masterpiece among masterpieces. Johannes Brahms, in a letter to Clara Schumann in June 1877, said about the Chaconne, "On one stave, for a small instrument, the man writes a whole world of the deepest thoughts and most powerful feelings. If I imagined that I could have created, even conceived the piece, I am quite certain that the excess of excitement and earth-shattering experience would have driven me out of my mind."

Violinist Joshua Bell has said the Chaconne is "not just one of the greatest pieces of music ever written, but one of the greatest achievements of any man in history. It's a spiritually powerful piece, emotionally powerful, structurally perfect." While numerous transcriptions have been made for keyboard, strings, chamber ensembles and even full orchestra (Leopold Stokowski), this transcription by world-renowned marimba artist, Mika Stoltzman, is the first-ever version written for solo marimba. A video of Stoltzman performing her stunning arrangement at the Purchase Performing Center in New York is available through the publisher's website: keisersouthernmusic.com.

BACH, J.S.
Ukena, Todd

ST585   Suite No. 1 in E Minor (Grade 5)

Movement titles: I. Praeludium, II. Allamande, III. Courante, IV. Sarabande, V. Bouree, VI. Gigue

BIZET, GEORGES
Maxey, Linda

ST893   Carmen Suite (Grade 5)

GIPSON, RICHARD

ST160   Prayer (Grade 4)

This beautiul piece for four-mallets is in ABA form. It is a wonderful contest or recital piece for those looking to balance more technical works with something more lyrical with rolling chord patterns under the melody.

GOMEZ, ALICE

ST483   Etude in d Minor (Grade 4)

Alice Gomez' "Etude in d Minor" will challenge the advancing marimbist with multiple compound meters and hemiola patterns.

ST505   Gitano (Gypsy) (Grade 4)

Gitano, meaning "Gypsy", is written in two movements and requires four mallets. Containing fast techincal sections with slow rubato sections interspersed and quick meter transitions, this is a wonderful recital or contest selection for the advancing marimbist.

SU41   Marimba Flamenca (Grade 5)

This piece for the advanced marimba player provides a wonderful opportunity to work on four-mallet technique and is a great selection for recital or contest. Written in an ABCA form, the first two sections are more technically challenging with the third section being a slow catabile, then a return to the original theme to the end.

SU824   Monarchs: Butterflies (Grade 3.5)

This light and airy piece in 6/8 time evokes the beautiful, but endangered, Monarch butterflies. Grade 3.5, Duration ca. 3'.

SU40   Scenes from Mexico (Grade 4)

This marimba solo suggests the ambiance and feeling of five different types of cultural locations in Mexico: The Village, The Church, The Cantina, The Playground, and The Fiesta.

SU428   Three Concert Pieces (Grade 3)

This collection of three independent pieces for marimba may be performed separately or in any combination that the performer prefers. Titles: 1. Celtic Rondo (two mallets, 2. Marimbula (two mallets), 3. Etude on C7 (four mallets)

GOMEZ/ RIFE

SU034   Mbira Song (Grade 3)

This enjoyable and challenging contest piece for marimba evokes the African Mbira, or "thumb piano" with its driving rhythmic ostinatos and pentatonic melodies.

ST695   Rain Dance (Grade 4)

This composition for solo marimba is a wonderful contest or recital piece for the advanced player, requiring three mallet work throughout, with some sections of four mallets. For an added optional effect, wrist bells may be worn throughout this piece.

GWIN, STEVEN

ST490   True Lover's Farewell (Grade 3)

A solo marimba setting of an Applachian folk song, dedicated by the composer to his wife Betsy.

JARVIS, DAVID E.

SU13   Jungle Walk (Grade 5)

This four-mallet solo for the advanced maribma player offers syncopated rhythms and multiple meters. It is a wonderful selection for contest or recital.

LARSON, KEITH

ST402   Suite Mexicana (Grade 3)

This three movement (fast-slow-fast), four mallet composition is an ideal contest or recital piece for intermediate players.

MAXEY, LINDA

SU313   Amazing Grace (Grade 3)

This beginning to intermediate arrangement is ideal for young players developing phrasing and legato technique on marimba.

SPEARS, JARED

ST749   Malletrix (Mallet Tricks) (Grade 3)

This two-mallet solo is a great contest or recital selection for the intermediate percussionist. Players will find both technically challenging sections and slower, lyrical parts.

UKENA, TODD

ST672   Colors (Grade 3)

This slow piece for four mallets explores harmonic progressions, and is a great option for practicing four mallet roll technique.

ST581   Lauren's Lullaby (Grade 4)

A single movement contest solo for marimba written in the style of a minuet.

ST673   Tempest (Grade 4)

This intermediate to advanced mallet solo features shifting accents over a "perpetual motion" sixteenth note pulse in the opening and closing sections. A more lyrical Adagio middle section employs rolls and dynamics, enhancing the longer melodic lines. Focus on sticking techniques and control are key aspects of the performance.

SOLO WITH PIANO

RIMSKY-KORSAKOV, NICOLAI
Maxey, Linda

SU293   Flight Of the Bumblebee (Grade 4)

This arrangement of Rimsky-Korsakov's *Flight of the Bumblebee* is provided by Linda Maxey. Linda Maxey also provides exercises to aid with the sticking.